Medicinal Melancholy

Mike R. Burns

For Me.

Follow Mike online:

Facebook: www.facebook.com/theinfernalether

Instagram: @theinfernalether

YouTube: www.youtube.com/mikeburns27

Tumblr: https://www.tumblr.com/blog/mike-r-burns

Melancholy is a beautiful lie. It will lure you in with romance in its eyes, promises on its lips, adventure on its tongue. You will fall, as everybody does, mouth agape with surprise when finally and inevitably you feel the knife in your back. Melancholy is falling in love with your pain. It usually happens out of necessity and desperation; when no one else is around to soothe you all you can do is rely on yourself, and loving the darkest parts of yourself seems like the only way you can live with yourself. Hell, no one else can, and it's not like you can get away from yourself. Well, you can, but you're not quite 'there' yet. But let Melancholy have its way with you and you will. It serves its purpose though, in small doses. It can give you perspective as few things can, but make no mistake, Melancholy is a love affair with Death and He likes to play for keeps.

Give me rain any day
Clouds thick with grey
Thunder and lightning
Wind, gentle, and sighing
Such beautiful melancholy
Soothes me wholly
I am taken
So much that I forget
For a few moments
That I'm
Still
Waiting

- *Vigil*

Of all the breathtaking art the universe has created, the most magnificent piece it ever has or will create is you.

- *Magnificent*

Breathe. Focus. Struggle on.

- *By Will Alone*

She could have anyone she wanted and more power to her, but what hurt the most was that I wasn't anyone to her anymore.

- *Evanescence*

Lately, I've been living rough
Because when I lost you
I lost my home

- *Vagrant Heart*

I am alone
But that's not why
I am lonely

I am lonely
Because I don't
Have you

If I never met you
My loneliness
Would have been bearable

But I did
And we made a life
Together as one

Now I am half of one
Trying to find
My other half within

I can only hope
That when I become one
You want us to become two

- *The Loneliest Number*

Where are you now?
What are you doing?
Are you thinking about me?
Probably not

I'm laying here wishing
I could turn and reach for you
And you would be there
But you don't want me

Oh, if loneliness could kill
I would have long succumbed
I hope you never know
What it's like to feel this way

- *Seriously, I Don't Recommend It*

All these things
I need to say aloud
I could tell anyone
Kind enough to listen
But it wouldn't help
Alleviate this malady
Or mean a goddamn thing
Because these things are
Only meant for you

If only your heart
Could hear them

- *Wasted Breath*

It always seemed strange to me that someone could die from a broken heart, but now, you could not convince me otherwise.

- *Live and Learn*

I know you are not the answer to all my problems, nor do I expect you to be. I just want you here, wanting me. That is all.

- Not-So-Simple Request

I am a mess of unfinished thoughts and burning questions. It's always been chaos inside my head, but you were the lantern in the dark. The ever-present constant I could rely on to guide me back home. Without you, I am lost and afflicted by a merciless fog, filled with inescapable horrors; all too eager to remind me of why I am here. Maybe I need to save myself and I will, but I just can't help but feel like I've been abandoned. Somehow I think I always knew that I would end up alone in the dark, with only my demons for company.

- *Sometimes It Sucks Being Right*

If you twist my arm, God does exist in a sense, but not how you think. God is not an omnipotent higher power, dictating how we live our lives and watching over us. God is the universe and everything in it. We are each a God as we each have the universe inside us. God as the universe is unthinking, unfeeling. It just is. And we are its consciousness. As we have billions of ideas that emanate and dissipate from our minds, as are we to the universe: the dreams of an eternally sleeping giant.

- *"Sooo, We're Gods, That Have The God Inside Us, But We Are Also Inside God?" "Yeah." "Whoa."*

I wish that instead of sleep we just died for the night. I don't want to dream, I don't want to be aware of anything, let alone the fact that I am alone. The relationship I have with Death is one of the very few things in this life that I'm afraid to commit to, but just for the night? That's fine with me.

- *A Dangerous Affair*

You were always destined to be immortal. Through my words, through the hearts of those you touched. Because of this, Death lost his claim to your soul.

- Them's the Breaks, Death

These nightmares are getting all too much. All I want when I wake up is for you to be here, so you can hold me and tell me everything is going to be okay. But you're not here and you don't care anymore.

I am become loneliness.

- *The Nightmares Came True*

Nothing and no one
Can fill the hole you left
It's reserved
For you and you alone
Oh sure, I can try
But it will always feel
Wrong

- *I'd Rather Be Empty Than Uncomfortable*

I feel manic
And chaotic
Swept up in the storm
My thoughts
Vague and shallow
Focus is waning
I can't stop moving
My skin is crawling
Paranoia abounds
You were my anchor
The sun shining through the clouds
The promise of a better tomorrow
Now
You're just...
Gone

- Reality Anxiety

I want to give you the world
Take you to
Every secret and
Secluded place we can find
I want to take you there
And kiss you
Away from eyes and opinions
Where it means everything
Where it truly matters
And just get lost
In each other
In passion
In lust
In love

- Get Lost

You are the light to my darkness
And my darkness is so
All consuming
That when you enter it
You burn like the sun
In all your blazing glory

- *Yin and Yang*

Invisible demons
Are reaching up from hell
Clawing away at my insides
Slowly, painfully, agonisingly
I am left with nothing but
Overwhelming melancholy
In these moments I wish
More than anything
For Death to embrace me
And take away all my pain

- Death's Unconditional Embrace

I wonder if you knew that tomorrow wasn't going to come, would you stop running away and run back into my arms?

- I Hope It Doesn't Take the End of the World

Individually my words
Scream out in pain
But if you piece them together
Into a mosaic
That resembles you?

Oh how they will sing
The most beautiful song of love

- *Mosaic*

Everything I do, no matter how I enjoy it, there is always something missing. I turn to you to share the moment, but you aren't there. And then, the moment is ruined.

- Ghost

Caught in the eye of the storm
It ravages and contorts my form
My spirit is slowly tattered and torn
And from this, hopelessness is born

- *Fear of Inevitability*

In the darkness
The cold caresses me
Jarring clarity
I am not calm
But begrudgingly content
The voices dull
I still feel them
But for the moment
This moment
Is mine
And mine alone.

- *Fleeting Reprieve*

I am being eaten alive
By memories of us
Who knew loneliness
Could cause such pain

My heart aches
With every solitary beat
My lungs suffocating without
You to breathe in

Damn you for being
So easy to love
Damn you for
Damning me

- *Damn It*

The older I get the more cynical and disillusioned about everything I become. Why is that? Am I just wired to have low expectations now? Maybe my brain just forgot how to be happy.

- *Just Smile and Nod*

Does no one take me seriously? I feel patronised and tolerated. Nothing I say is considered unless someone else is of the same opinion. No wonder I find solace in solitude. Though I suppose it's fair, it's not like I take them seriously either.

- *People Suck*

It's hard not to question myself, not to feel pathetic. Anyone else would've moved on by now. Am I just a joke? The example people give when they say, "You know who's sad?" I know I shouldn't believe anymore, yet I do, stronger than ever. I feel it like it's in my bones. I weather the daily humiliation, the torture, the shame, believing that it will all be worth it one day. I know that it is my choice but my heart cannot bear the thought of giving up and that is why I endure.

- *Tragic*

This life is just an insult to me now, being made to stand here with smiles and laughter, stuffing down anything that is more than friendly. In my head, I imagine grabbing you by the shoulders, shaking you, screaming at you to tell your heart to remember who I am! Tell it to let me back in again! But you are just blank, like a doll, no reaction. The loneliness creeps in, slowly encasing everything in ice. I am frozen. And so I continue to smile and laugh, because what else can I do?

- *Resignation*

Am I just an annoying fly that you absent-mindedly swat away whenever I come close?

- *Morty*

When you see people in love
Or hear a song about people in love
Do I still come into your mind?
When you think of love
Do you still think about what we had?
When you think of me do you think
Maybe, one day?

- *Just Not Today*

The more you push me away, the more my resolve is emboldened. I suppose I like the challenge, facing impossible odds and still winning the day. Is there a more romantic tale? The man who won the heart of the woman who said no? And what greater tragedy than the man who continuously tries only to fail? Either I win your heart or a lifetime of unbridled melancholy; there is no in-between.

- *When I Go All In...*

I don't want to see the sky no more
Give me dark clouds forevermore
I've lived in melancholy for so long
And always found comfort in a sad song
I can only taste bittersweet
Kept alive with memories on repeat
No mercy for my soul
A supermassive black hole

- *Everything and Nothing*

People are not equipped to listen these days. Sure they understand the concept of listening, but only so they can figure out when it's their turn to talk again, about themselves. The overwhelming narcissism of the population is astounding. Everything always relates back to the self in some way, and they *will* find a way. No one is willing to offer their kindness or time unless they have something to gain from it. It's hard not to feel lonely in a world where you are the opposite of all these things.

- *Yes, You Matter, But So Does Everyone Else*

Since my life has spiralled out of control I've struggled to come up with a way to explain how I feel about everything, to describe this depressing and almost surrealistic existence I now lead. I suffered through mediocrity from the moment I became aware only to one day find her and be woken up to some of the greatest things life had to offer. Then just when I thought life couldn't get any better, I was taken and beaten into submission. Expected to return to mediocrity and ignore that I had shared something so special with someone, almost to the point where I questioned if it ever happened at all, like it was some fever dream. When I see her she meets me with indifference, no trace left of the warmth in her eyes I once coveted. It's a strange thing to feel like you've lost everything but at the same time question whether you had anything at all.

- *DoublePlusGood*

New year, new you? For how long? A month? A week? Look, just stop. You owe it to yourself to set new standards; commit to ongoing change, growth, and education. Change, grow, and learn because it will make you happy. Because you want the best life you can give yourself. Never stop trying, again and again, tomorrow is a new day. Take small steps and stop putting so much pressure on yourself; not only will your failures be infinitely less crushing, you will learn and achieve more than you ever dreamed. You are worthy.

- Chase The Journey

If I died tomorrow, how would you mourn me? As someone who realised they have lost their soul mate? As your closest friend? As the father of your child? Maybe all of the above? Or a chapter finally closed?

- *Multiple Choice*

You could be with anyone and only be thinking about them. I could be with anyone and only be thinking about you.

- *Distracted*

When you touched my heart for the first time, when the fires of love and lust burned so passionately in your blood, your fingerprints were seared into the delicate flesh, forever marking it as yours. You changed the rhythm of its beat with overwhelming pain and pleasure. It has an intensity that never yields and deafeningly fills the silence.

So no, you never leave my thoughts.

- *Always On My Mind*

It's not that I actively avoid human contact. There's a difference between avoidance and not seeking it out. I just prefer my own company, that's all.

- *Sweet Solitude*

If you think life is disappointing, you ask too much from it. You may have earned your right to be here, but that doesn't mean it's going to be easy. Life doesn't owe you shit. It's been survival of the fittest since before you were conceived. If you can't keep up, you'll be left behind. Pick yourself up, dust yourself off, do something about it, and keep moving forward. Life sucks; the sooner you accept it, the better.

- They Pulled The Wool Over Your Eyes, But You Left It There

All I ever wanted growing up was to be needed. I got what I wanted, but it was never enough. When I met you I realised that I needed to be wanted and how real, fulfilling, and intoxicating that difference is. To know that someone has chosen you above all others, not out of compulsion, just pure and considered choice. That is the most powerful gesture you can ever experience.

- *Perspective Changes Everything*

I hate these awkward silences. Especially when they come about because finally, after much self deliberation, I grew the balls to have a confrontation. I didn't want this, but it's done, it's been said, let's move on. Why must we dwell on these things? I've never understood human kind's incessant need to dwell, percolate, and stew on bullshit that makes us unhappy. Is it because we latch on to the fact that we are actually feeling something other than cold indifference for once and want to hold on to that feeling for as long as possible before it dissipates into the ether? Why can't we choose love and understanding? If that's too strange due to lack of experience, why can't we practise it? Use confrontation as a stepping stone back to love? We humans are much more complicated than we need to be.

- *It's Not Rocket Science*

These nights where I can't sleep, head in my hands, tearing myself to shreds, the nights when I need you the most, these are the nights I wanna die. If Death appeared at that moment and offered his hand I'd happily take it, and plead for him to take me away. Until morning anyway.

- Death Must Hate Me, I'm Such A Tease

No matter how good the story is, if the ending sucks, that's all you are going to remember.

- *That's Why It Can't End Yet*

Isn't it such grandiose irony, that the fulfilling of your dreams has become my nightmare? I know I should be happy that you are happy, and to a certain extent I am, but there are few things I can think of that are more torturous than this inescapable fate.

- *Where's My Silver Lining?*

Sleep for me is always hard-fought-for now. And when the battle has been won, I'm rewarded with horrific matinees of all that haunts me.
Such hollow victory.

- *Where's My "Monster"?*

Life is like a wish granted by a twisted genie. Sure, they will grant it, but it will not come without irony; for all the pleasure you experience, you will endure twice as much pain. I wonder if we knew, would we still make the wish?

- I Sure As Hell Wouldn't Be Wishing For His Freedom. Prick.

These are the only options in regards to life problems: deal with them, accept them, or let them go. Anything else is a waste of energy, encouraging you to nurture pain and stress.

- *It's One Thing To Know, Another To Apply*

If you are going to use obscenities, commit to that shit. Don't bitch out and put little fucking asterisks in place of vowels, don't bleep it out. Self-censoring and catering to delicate sensibilities takes away any and all credibility you may have had or gotten. Yes, we knew what you meant, but now we think less of you for saying it.

- Was That Too Cunty?

Of the same dark cloth we are cut, both of us willing slaves and conduits of written expression. 'Tis ironic shame that each are we hesitant to immerse ourselves in each other's divine calling, as they are concomitant of our failings to the other.

- *Star-Crossed*

Insanity is the result of having the validity of your heart's lament constantly being called into question.

- *So, "Gaslighting" Is A Fun Term I Learned Today*

I always dreamed of having a family of my own, one that I chose to have because the one that was forced upon me was less than lacking. Who of us can say that we made our dream a reality? Not many can, but I did. I realised my dream, and it was a family born of love! One more thing that is a rarity, in these days of lust and infidelity.

I feel so out of touch with the world now my dream has been shattered. I've been left behind and I am drowning. I'm losing the will to fight for my self. I just want to close my eyes and let the cold, dark abyss swallow me whole.

- *Dramatic Much?*

Sometimes I long for the days of old, where you could just choose a direction, walk, and stumble into adventures that distract you from all that is dragging you down.

- *Born Too Late*

Fumbling
Dazzling lights
Humbling
Freedom
Ecstasy
Succumb
Journey and toil

- Drunken Poetry Part Un

Crackle and buzz
Against a midnight hue
Dark and light
Such a romantic cue
Taste of the night
This exquisite moment

- *Drunken Poetry Part Deux*

Stars
There is no pressure
To be anything
They just are

- Drunken Poetry Part Trois

Some days I think I could just die. Not because I want to kill myself, but because my body is on the brink of just shutting down from simple lack of will to live.

- Death Is Whispering Sweet Nothings Again

It doesn't matter how many pills they give me, how many times I shrink my head, or how fulfilling my life becomes; without you I will never be okay. It's not about whether or not I can let go, or being obsessed, or any other kind of demeaning reason. It meant something to me, plain and simple. When did giving a shit suddenly go out of fashion?

- Love? Ha! How Passé.

It's become increasingly apparent that *forever* is no longer a part of your vocabulary, but I am becoming increasingly starved of you. So I propose this; allow me this moment; allow me this moment to sate my hunger, to devour everything that you are. And maybe, just maybe, you can find time and inclination enough to grant me more than just one.

- *Moments In Time*

Where am 'I'?
A spectre in the void
An echo of something that was never found

- Existence Is Fickle

Sensuous intrigue in her chest
Alluring lips moist with attitude
She is mystery and freedom
Jesus! This chick has me like no one will
She is poetry

- Fridge Magnets

I don't ask you about your day or what you're doing anymore, because I just assume you're lying, whether you are or not and I know you have before. I guess I should thank you for lying, but is it to save my feelings or save you from dealing with them? Well, here's the thing, it doesn't even matter in the end, because I'm fucked either way.

- *This Is Why We Can't Be Friends*

I hold this pain dearly. Not out of spite, not out of stubbornness, but because it means everything to me. I need to know that I meant more to you than a phase you went through. That all those moments were more than just fever dreams. That you still think of me before you go to sleep. That some part of you misses feeling my breath on your neck, and my heart beating against your back. That you miss being more than passing ships in the night. That you even miss me at all.

- I Think It Would Destroy Me More If You Did

I feel so brittle, just barely holding together. My mind has been arrested and held in contempt. This emptiness aches, more and more, crying out to be numbed. This self-hate is like acid, overflowing, longing to spill out and drown everyone in it. There is no such thing as absolution, you either survive or you don't and it's a death sentence either way.

- *Does My Trauma Turn You On?*

I always thought true love would save me
Imagine my surprise when I realised
It was
Killing
Me

- *Typical*

Looking at photos of us preparing for the next chapter of our lives, we looked so in love, like nothing could ever tear us apart. It's hard to reconcile, now that everything is in ruins and you being unrecognisable. If it meant anything to you like you say it did, there's no way you could have simply walked away like you did.

- Don't Fucking Lie To Me

Why am I the one left here to rot? When all I had to give was love? I'm plagued by insomnia, while you sleep soundly. I'm shedding tears, and you're having the time of your life. You say you have an infinite love for everyone, not just one; well what's so special about that? You tell me I fell in love with a lie; is that how you can justify all that you destroyed? Isn't it funny how life changes? How forever was just a slip of the tongue? How you walked away and you never looked back? How even now I still love you with everything that I am?

What a laugh.

-*Why Couldn't You Just Kill Me Instead?*

Some nights, much like tonight, I wish I could run away with Death and never come back. Some nights, much like tonight, I hate that I'm responsible, and care about more than myself. If it wasn't for her, sleeping soundly and unaware, tonight I would call Death to take me away. I don't wanna feel anymore because I just can't stop. I know he could take all my pain away if I was selfish and thought only of myself. I wanna hate, but I just can't, I'm wired only to love. Apparently inside every cynic is a disappointed idealist and an idealist is an optimist who was let down too many times. An absurdist is a cynic who realises nothing matters anyway and when the absurdist can't find context in existentialism anymore, all that remains and holds any comfort is oblivion.

- Nothing Truly Matters In the End

Whenever I allow myself even a minute to let the full gravity of all that has happened, all that has been lost to wash over me, my insides turn to ice, and I feel like I'm drowning. How fucked is that?

- *Just Like Going Home*

I wonder is it karma that we now find ourselves in the same position that we joked would happen to others, but never us?

- *Ego Is A Dirty Word*

I know, I know now where it all went wrong. It was the day you decided I wasn't worth your help. The years I spent running from my own demons, so I could help you battle yours. Then they finally were beaten into submission, that's when you turned on me
My demons ended up being more than I could handle alone, I needed your help and you despised that
I was weak while you were now strong. I'd spent so long fighting your demons, I'd forgotten how to fight my own. I was being overcome and you turned your back on me. You got out alive, so it should've been easy for me! Right?!

Oh, what evil seeds are sown, when we forget we didn't get where we are alone.

- *No Excess Baggage*

Wanna know the surest way to eviscerate yourself? Facebook memories.

- *Modern Day Hara-Kiri*

Will I ever be free of this yoke of pain? No matter how much joy the day's events may bring, I always pay a heavy price and find it hard not to regret having done anything at all.

- *Chronic Pain In My Arse*

While time does not heal
It does bring perspective
The hurt never goes away
But it stops being a reason to hide
The blinders are removed and
There are now new paths to follow
Almost like a spell has been broken
And you are seeing the world with fresh eyes
While things aren't perfect
They are better than they were yesterday
As bittersweet as it is
If nothing else, it's a reason to finally smile
Because it means you've hit rock bottom
And now the only way to go is up

- I Might Be Broken, But I Ain't Dead Yet

I am of the opinion that without melancholy you cannot see the true beauty of the world, or everyone and everything in it. How can you know the true and personal value of someone or something without knowing the sadness you would feel were you to lose them? Unfortunately, for some of us, the resulting melancholy is all too consuming.

- *Enlightenment, Very Rarely, Breeds Happiness*

I feel like I'll never shake this idea that *I'm not good enough*. Trying to find love for yourself when it never existed is like trying to quench your thirst from a dry well. If I cannot find love for myself, am I doomed to repeating the same mistakes? I tried to swear off love, but I yearn so deeply for it. Will I yearn less if I learn to love myself? Would it just be easier to redouble my efforts in closing off my heart, tearing it off my face, and burying it deep in the dark of my chest? The evil in my brain is almost deafening, screaming oppressively that this is my life, and I don't deserve any better. I am unloveable and not worth a damn from anyone. I am too weak to retort and the past is irrefutable evidence. I am left with two choices, accept my fate or die.

- *'Broken' Doesn't Even Begin To Describe Me*

It's amazing what can happen when we act in spite of our anxieties.

- *Shouting Down The Abyss*

I am not one of those writers that consistently churn out work every day. I've never worked like that. I mostly write when I need to drive some demon from my mind. Sometimes that can force me to be prolific, but when my demons are dormant, I am so utterly uninspired. To force myself to write any other way would be a lie. And yet, because of this, I feel shunned by my peers, which ironically is why is started writing in the first place.

- Defiant Till The End

Suffering may, in fact, be ultimately pointless, but tell me what aspect of existence isn't! If you can assign meaning to something to make it worthwhile for *you*, and can learn and grow from it, or at the very least have something useful become of it, then even suffering has its purpose.

- *It's All An Illusion Anyway*

Intentions originally thought to be good, rarely ever end up as such.

- *Please, Just Don't.*

It would be a fucking miracle if I could wake up one day and not wish I hadn't.

- *Pipe Dream*

I think I latched onto melancholy because otherwise, I am empty. I was never really taught to cultivate anything else; melancholy or nothingness, those were my choices and everything else was a lie. I tried faking it, but I never really made it. And now as I enter the next third of my life, I realise how much I have lost because of that.

- *There's No Do-Over's Man!*

I'm still waiting to happen across the wisdom my confusion is said to bring.

- *Forever Waiting For Some Damn Thing Or Another*

I hate small talk and I am terrible at it. Not because I don't have the capacity for it, but because I just don't care. Unless I'm having a conversation about something important and meaningful, my mind is going to wander and I'm just not going to listen. If I see someone I know in the street, I will usually avoid talking to them because the 5 minutes we do talk is just going to be a waste of our collective time. So know that if I do make the effort for small talk with you, you're one of my favourite people, and it's your company that I crave, regardless of the conversation had.

- *Playing Favourites*

I'm a mess. I only make tentative plans or goals for the future and I feel so trapped when things are set in stone. I need to reserve the right to back out of something at any given time. I don't like working to a checklist or to a deadline. If I am forced to do anything I will unconsciously rebel against it.

- *You Sweet Summer Child. GROW THE FUCK UP!*

I am fated, despite my best intentions, to not only cause myself infinite unhappiness, but also inflict pain on those I care about. It seems I am best suited to cutting myself off from the world and not imposing myself upon it.

- *Bad Luck Charm*

This oppressive aura
Will be the death of me
To be sure

Nary a moment of clarity
A blinding haze
Horrific familiarity

My desire to be more
Is strong, but weathered
I am exhausted to my core

I unravel for days at a time
Like I'm being punished
For an unknown crime

I feel more dead than alive
And every day is a struggle
Just to survive

- *Survive*

If there is one thing you should know about me, it is that I am compelled to say the things that are on my mind, especially if they are positively inclined. Nothing is more frustrating to me than to feel like I need to hold back all the good things I want to say to someone for fear that they will retreat due to preconceived misconceptions. Again, I am wired to love, and also to not be able to hide it. I don't want anything in return for my admirations except to see the light in someone's eyes from the flames that are warming their heart.

- Stoker

How is it that even now after all this time and all this pain I still want you? But I know that it's different now, I'm not consumed by hollow unrequited love. I am brimming with excitement, as much as I would be at the beginning of a new love and I am ravenous, so much so that I want to devour everything about you once more. I can't even sit next to you without struggling to contain my boyish glee, my heart pounding, and my thoughts ablaze. Patience has never been my strong suit, you know this well; I want it all and I want it now. Show me mercy and sate my hunger.

- Come On, You Know You Want To

I tried to fight, I tried letting go, I tried moving on. When nothing worked before, why is it when I have tried doing nothing I've been brought back to you? Is it manifestation? Every time I looked to another, wishing they were you? I know I'm getting ahead of myself, but I can't help it. Patience is a virtue, but it was never one of mine and especially now that I have a penchant for impulsivity, being around you is driving me crazy for all new reasons. Yes, the sadness is still there and I'm glad because it serves as a reminder: to never take you or anything else for granted ever again.

- Never Again, Not Even For A Minute, Will I Let You Wonder

There is an infinite amount of knowledge and wisdom in pain, but only if you have the courage to face it.

- *Turn And Face The Pain*

When there is silence between us, how is it the air is empty, but so heavily pregnant at the same time? Will one of us ever have the courage to break that silence and give birth to truth and reality?

- *Say Something!*

Bright, overcast, and rainy days always seem to present the world in all its beauty and melancholic splendour. The many types of vibrant greens, highlighted with delicate dew drops like silvery diamonds. It seems so fantastical and otherworldly. These are the days I live for.

- Nature Can Be Such A Turn On Sometimes. Damn.

The only true fate is that which you decide for yourself.

- *Plain And Simple*

I am so good at hurting myself
That it makes sense
Hurting others comes naturally

- *Hurt*

You are an enigma, even though I know you better than most. Once I thought I had unlocked all your mysteries, now only to find you wrapped in layers anew. I want more than anything, the chance to peel them away again.

- *That Peelin' Feelin'*

The past is nothing more than lessons to be learned, rather than irrefutable proof of the future.

- *Stop Over-thinking It!*

I remember all the promises you made and the fire in your eyes when you made them known. I was overwhelmed by the heat of your conviction, so much so that now you're gone the cold bites that much harder.

- *Frostbite*

Things that truly matter take time. There is meaning and fulfilment attached to the toil; it is an investment towards something greater than yourself. And that in itself is eternally rewarding, more so than anything else.

- *Aim Big, Start Small*

To react and react alone is to say without a doubt, you have lost control. But to respond instead and then adapt? That is true mastery of self.

- Emotions Aren't Inherently Bad, But They Can Lead You Astray

Oh little pill, little pill, work your magic for me. Save me once again from the demons in my soul, so that I may find solace, however fleeting, in the sleep of the dead.

- Prayer

Whenever I stumble across
A thought of you
My world stops
And I have to remind myself to breathe again

- *Insert Cliché Here*

There is a fear that grips my heart
I am afraid if you come to find
That you still have love for me
You will be too stubborn to show it

- *Prove Me Wrong, Please?*

Is it so wrong that I want the cliché romantic comedy love story? I want the grand gesture of love, I want to feel like I am your whole world and you don't care who knows it, in fact, you want everyone to know it. I don't give a shit how that sounds, just like anyone in the history of existence I just want to feel important and I want to feel the most important to you.

- "I Mean, Did You Really See A Future With This Girl?" "Like, With Jetpacks."

4 years old today
4 years gone today
A life stolen
A new life in its place
You changed our world
With your sweet, innocent face
Though your eyes stayed closed
Ours were forever opened

Your name is scarred
On both halves of my heart
The memories seared in my brain
Never far when I want to be close to you
My lips still feel the smooth cold of your brow
And even now it's hard to reconcile the truth
That I will never have the chance to say
Happy birthday Dante

- Dante Nalin Burns 19.06.2013

Believe me when I say you are my everything. Not because I can't live without you, it's obvious that I can, but because I think about you before I sleep, and again when I wake; you're always with me in everything I do. Many would call it obsession and so what? Who doesn't obsess about what or who they love? Is it really a crime to have so much love in your heart? The only crime I see here is having to silence your heart. What is in your heart? Can you tell me? Have you silenced yours so long now that it speaks in whispers too low for you to hear? I remember when my words used to bring you to tears, tears of love, and joy. Now my words only seem to induce indifference. Is it that in silencing your heart it decided to stop listening? I know you know what we had was special, but like all the others we weren't immune to losing our way. It was a lesson we both needed to learn so we could be born again as something incredible. I know most would prescribe time as the remedy for this malady, but we both know that patience is not a virtue we hold dear. We are impulsive, passionate, and hedonistic; time is not a friend of ours. We were made to dive headlong into adventure, consequences be damned! Won't you take my hand now and join me on our next adventure together? This time it will be born from true and conscious love! It will be an adventure that will last a lifetime and many more to come, an adventure that exists here in the now. Take my hand and let's leave the past behind, we shall turn and side by side face the unknown together.

- *All Is Not Lost*

When you are truly starved for affection, you will seek it out in the strangest of arms.

- *Lovesick*

Say all the things that are bouncing around in your mind no matter how stupid or hurtful. Say them so not only you, but everyone else can hear how they sound out loud, because how else do you expect to learn anything about yourself, how you fit into the world, and whether you need to change when you only have yourself as a sounding board? Keeping these things to yourself is the surest way to reinforcing ignorance and negativity.

- Leave Nothing Left Unsaid

When you are desperate for affection and try to fill that need by fucking strangers or people you know are bad for you, you are gonna have a bad time. I liken it to buying steak. You're generally used to getting a nice porterhouse or even a rump steak, but when you're kind of poor you go for the cheapest option. The cut which no one asked for or wanted: the sizzle steak. It's just there, waiting, and counting on the desperation to set in. You take it home, try cooking it, and it's just a horrible experience. You're feeling disappointed already and you haven't even started to eat it. It cooks much too quickly and you almost burn it because it's not made for cooking at the high temperatures you're used to. Then when you go to eat it, it has no taste or substance, and it's just dry and chewy. And while you're lamenting every bite, it's gone before you even realise. You're left feeling empty, guilty, and disillusioned because you were weak and decided to cheap out. Sure you had steak, but was it really worth it?

- Don't Act Like You Don't Know What I'm Talking About

Love isn't easy, if it is you're doing it wrong and it is going to fail. Why? Because you are compromising not only your beliefs, but also yourself, for the sake of harmony. This is how relationships stagnate; you are killing your own passion for the sake of being agreeable. You can see this for yourself; look at all the relationships you are exposed to, and figure out which ones are the strongest and the happiest. I guarantee you that it is the couples who are always butting heads, as long as they also have the capacity to realise that they can be wrong. This fosters respect, which in turn stokes the fires of love, but also provides room for growth. These basic tenets are the foundation of unbreakable relationships.

- Be True To Yourself, In All Things

The Abyss is stealing my sleep.

- *Bloodshot*

I'm too scared to sleep, but it hurts too much to be awake. Why isn't *this* the dream?

- *Insomnia*

Those who do not know true and brutal pain will not know the universe, and the universe does not suffer ignorance.

- *Choose Courage, Discover Life*

The brain can be amazing (although oftentimes it can be quite the oafish dullard); sometimes it can save its own life. You could spend many nights cradled in the arms of Death, having him whisper sweet nothings into your ear about how he will take you away from here and you will never feel pain again. Every night your brain succumbing all the more to his incessant seduction, only to one day wake up and have your brain say "You know what? I think I'm done. This has been going on too long and I need a change of scenery. Fuck off out my bed and outta my house Death."

It's not like the pain or the trauma has gone, it's very much still there and prominent as ever, but for the first time in a long time it's not dragging me down. It is a part of me now, not the other way around, and I'm no longer scared of this new life.

- *Self-Preservation*

Always assume that your partner might leave you tomorrow; never try to explain that fear away. Use that fear to keep your passion alive; treat every day like it's your courting days. Never stop the chase, because the moment you do is the moment it all starts to fall apart.

- Love Is A Goddamn Privilege, Not A Right. So Fucking Treat It That Way.

To give of yourself, when you truly feel like there is nothing left inside you to give. That, I feel, is the true meaning of love, strength, character, and compassion.

- To Live Is To Give

Oh, how fickle my muse is. I can always call on her in despair, but in joy, she is flaky at best.

- *Bitch Just Loves To See Me Squirm*

Love without effort is a lie and all lies are brought to bear eventually. If you don't try and win your love every single day then one day someone else will win your love. You are not owed anything in this life, especially love.

Stop acting like you are.

- Earn It

When your head and heart are exploding at the same time, and you're sitting there staring at nothing in silence, because there are no voices in your head telling you what to do. You can hear just barely audible whispers, moving further, and further away. They're like rats jumping off a sinking ship, like they know you're a lost cause and they abandon you without a backward glance. Those moments are the hardest to come back from.

- Rats

My body aches for things
It does not understand
My heart craves everything
It cannot have
And my head? Well,
It just doesn't know anymore
I've put my soul on the line
In more ways than one
And every time I lost a little more
The world turns more black than grey
It only takes a moment to relive a lifetime
A moment to relive what felt like a lifetime
And the tsunami that I ride
Brings overwhelming transcendence
All I can do is close my eyes
Hold my breath
My teeth are ready to explode
All I have to do is let go
Just let go
I can't let go
Why can't I let go?
I am covered in green
And filled with scarlet
Burning alive in silence
Am I the fool and I don't know it?
Stifled laughter out of earshot
Or am I little more than a grain of sand?
Just another, lost in a sea of others
I would've hoped I was more
But alas! I am caught in your wake
With a fleeting glance over your shoulder
You catch my gaze for a moment
Then you turn and disappear into the night

- *Return To The Ether*

My thoughts race
Too many to make sense
Confusion interlaced
With doubt makes me dense

Damaged, broken
I'm trying to heal
But crippled by words unspoken
I don't want to be me anymore

The one that got me here
Turn my back, settle the score
I hate him. I despise and loathe
I'll leave him for dead

Leave myself exposed
Start again, clean slate
I want to be free, I will be
Free of this poisonous state

I'll find me, you'll see
I need to now, I don't want to wait
But I can't escape the journey
My fate is my own to create

- Keep Pushing Through

The veil finally lifted and he saw. He saw the horrors, the hell that he himself had created, and he wept.

- *A Dark Epiphany*

I am a mess of good intentions
And contradictions
Every step uncertain and questioned
I'm sorry for being sorry
For wearing my heart on my face
My burden to bear
I'm high maintenance
You'll regret my acquaintance
I try to embrace the unknown
But I can't leave unanswered questions alone
I'm my own worst enemy
I'll be the death of you
You'll see

- Stunted And Irresponsible

There isn't one person in this world that isn't a product of their upbringing or their situation, but here's the thing, you've got two choices: you either become affected by it or you become effective because of it.

Which will you choose?

- *Life is Hard, Suck It Up Princess*

Printed by Libri Plureos GmbH in Hamburg, Germany